CHASE O'SHIELDS

I. Don't. Care. (Mostly)

My Secret to Managing Stress.

First published by Chase O'Shields 2023

Copyright © 2023 by Chase O'Shields

All rights reserved. No part of this publication may be reproduced, stored or transmitted in any form or by any means, electronic, mechanical, photocopying, recording, scanning, or otherwise without written permission from the publisher. It is illegal to copy this book, post it to a website, or distribute it by any other means without permission.

Chase O'Shields asserts the moral right to be identified as the author of this work.

First edition

This book was professionally typeset on Reedsy.
Find out more at reedsy.com

To my lovely therapist–extraordinaire wife who always supports me, my endlessly supportive family, and my friends who've tolerated my ridiculous quirks, this book about mental health is dedicated to you. You're the sanity in my insanity!
With love, Chase

Contents

Preface

Unlocking the I Don't Care Mindset

What even is this book!? It's your passport to a richer, more balanced life.

Your Roadmap Awaits:
This book isn't a pit-stop; it's your travel guide. Swap quick fixes for lasting metamorphosis. With this book as your trusty compass, explore the terrain of mental well-being with renewed vigor.

From Theory to Practice:
Don't just read—act. Arm yourself with strategies born from the real world, ready to weave into your daily grind. Each page brings a fresh perspective, a new challenge, and a practical step to own your mental wellness.

Interactive Pit Stops:
Jazz up your jaunt with exercises that aren't just fillers—they're the main event. Pause, reflect, and embed the "I Don't Care" ethos into your psyche. Remember, it's also how you get there, not just the destination.

Champion Your Mind:

There's a treasure within you. Unearth it, polish it, and let it shine. Embrace the notion of not caring and watch stress and anxiety fade, making room for pure, unadulterated joy.

Deep Dive Ahead:

Get ready to plunge! Each chapter offers a deeper layer, a richer texture, peeling back the curtain on life-changing mental health insights. Connect the dots and find your path to a life brimming with purpose and discovery.

Before we plunge further, here's a quirky tidbit about this book: I LOVE lists! They're like little mental snack packs. Tasty, quick, and oh-so-satisfying.

The Role of Lists:

1. **Clarity**: Lists offer a clear and organized way to present information. They help break down complex concepts into digestible pieces, making them easier to understand.
2. **Quick Comprehension**: In our fast-paced world, lists provide a quick and efficient way to grasp essential ideas. Readers can pinpoint key takeaways without wading through lengthy paragraphs.
3. **Actionable Insights**: Lists often contain actionable steps and tips that you can implement immediately, enhancing the practicality of the content.

So, every time you spot a list, know that there's a nugget of wisdom waiting to be unearthed. Dig in!

What to Expect: The Complete Itinerary

As you embark on this exploration, we've designed a reading experience that's both engaging and illuminating. Here's what you can anticipate:

Guides:

- Practical Guides: Some chapters boast tailored exercises to guide you through self-assessment activities. Dive deep, and let the principles seep in.

Topical Lists:

- Quick Summaries: Want a snapshot of the essentials? We got you! Topical lists encapsulate core concepts, making retention a breeze.

Action Plans:

- Your Blueprint: These are your roadmaps to a transformed life. Follow these actionable steps, infusing the book's wisdom into your daily existence.
- You'll start to see these more towards the end when we start trying to bring it all back together.

Key Takeaways:

- Chapter Highlights: As you wrap up each chapter, take a moment to reflect on its essence. We've handpicked the gold nuggets, presenting them in succinct takeaways.

Sub-Chapters:

- Bite-Sized Wisdom: For every chapter, there's a sub-chapter: a distilled version that breaks material down into more digestible and reader-friendly bits. Perfect for those on the go or for a quick recap.
- We will call these "Unravels"

The Complexities of the Mind and Mental Health: A Note

In the literary symphony that is my book on (mostly) mental health, the quartet of words—prioritize, self-care, emotional, and resilience—grace the pages like a well-rehearsed ensemble. Why, you might wonder? Well, let me share a secret—they're the versatile actors in this mental health drama, donning various costumes and striking multiple poses to create a captivating narrative.

First up, "Prioritize" leads the charge, like the director of a play ensuring everything stays on track. It reminds us to set our mental health center stage, but it doesn't stop there. Oh no, it teams up with "Self-care" to become the dynamic duo— like Batman and Robin of well-being. Together, they shout, "Prioritize self-care!" urging us to give ourselves top billing in the grand production of life.

Meanwhile, "Emotional" emerges as the scene-stealer, delivering soliloquies on the vast spectrum of feelings that color our existence. It dances with "Self-care," forming a tango of emotional self-care, reminding us to cherish our emotional well-being as an essential subplot in our story.

Now, here's where the plot thickens. "Resilience" enters, wearing its armor of strength and determination. It partners with "Emotional" to create the powerful "Emotional resilience," highlighting that acknowledging our feelings is the first step toward building the unshakable armor of mental fortitude.

But the real magic happens when all four words come together to create harmony. "Prioritize self-care for emotional resilience" becomes the showstopper, demonstrating that placing well-being at the forefront isn't just a one-man act; it's a well-choreographed dance of priorities.

As the book unfolds, these words perform a ballet of meaning, illustrating that prioritizing self-care isn't just about face masks and bubble baths (although those are lovely too!). It's about nurturing your emotional landscape, building the resilience to withstand life's plot twists, and writing a mental health story that deserves a standing ovation.

As a quick tidbit about myself, music holds a special place in my heart. I'm an enthusiast of all genres, and what's remarkable is my ability to recall lyrics from songs dating back more than two decades. To give you a glimpse into my mind and shed light on the power of repetition:

Imagine your brain as a jukebox; the more you play a song, the more you remember its lyrics, and this concept holds true for other things too. In the world of learning (not caring, included), repeating ideas is like catchy tunes that stick in your head. It's like your brain's way of saying, "Let's remember this!" When you repeat something, your brain strengthens the connections linked to that information, making it easier to recall. Just like you can't forget your favorite song's chorus, you can use repetition to remember essential mental health strategies. But remember, don't overdo it; too much repetition can be dull. We'll show you how to strike the right balance, using repetition effectively to create a mental health playlist that sticks in your mind. So, get ready to groove your way to better mental well-being!

On top of those amazing words above, you'll find an additional smidge of repetition in this book around concepts. Why? Because life's lessons are like a plate of spaghetti—everything's interconnected. And as we untangle one noodle of wisdom, you'll see it's linked to another, and another.

If you sense déjà vu, it's not a glitch in the matrix; it's by design. Embrace it!

So, as you read on, let these words take center stage because they're not just words; they're the protagonists in your mental health journey, ready to paint a permanent masterpiece on the canvas of your life.

The Aspiration

My hope is that as you jump headfirst into the pages of this book, certain ideas will captivate you, provoke thought, or resonate deeply. Allow yourself the opportunity to explore these sparks further. Ask: How does this align with my personal course? Could this insight be beneficial for me? I've entered into a personal voyage of introspection to understand the intricacies of my own psyche, the reasons behind my thoughts, and the elements that make me who I am. Self-reflection is immensely empowering, and the hike to self-awareness is the most rewarding adventure you can set sail on.

And just like that, you're on the threshold of a life where you not only reclaim your peace but also rediscover the joys of saying, "I Don't Care." All aboard this enlightening voyage! Prepare to make some waves and perhaps even meet a friendly whale or two along the way.

x

1

Introduction

Understanding the Concept

In today's fast-paced and demanding world, the concept of "I Don't Care" represents a profound and liberating mindset shift. It's important to clarify that this does not advocate indifference or neglect. Instead, it's a conscious and deliberate choice to take control of our lives and well-being.

Reframing Priorities

At its core, it encourages us to reevaluate our priorities. It prompts us to step back from the constant stream of expectations and demands that society places on us and ask a fundamental question: "What actually matters?" This inner look allows us to differentiate between what is essential and what is merely noise in our lives.

Empowering Self-Care

This thought process empowers us to prioritize ourselves

and our mental well-being. It's a declaration that we refuse to be burdened by trivial matters that can consume our time and energy. Instead, we choose to invest our resources in activities, relationships, and pursuits that nurture our emotional, psychological, and social well-being.

Setting Boundaries

Embracing the art means setting healthy boundaries. It involves saying "no" when necessary, not out of selfishness but as an act of self-preservation. This boundary-setting enables us to protect our mental health and preserve our energy for what truly matters.

Finding Balance

This can promote balance in our lives. It encourages us to avoid the trap of over-committing and spreading ourselves too thin. By focusing on what genuinely contributes to our well-being, we strike a harmonious balance between our responsibilities and our personal needs.

It is a conscious choice to reclaim our agency in a world filled with noise and distractions. It's a declaration that we value our mental health and are committed to nurturing it by paying attention to what truly matters. This stance empowers us to lead more fulfilling and emotionally balanced lives.

The Importance of Mental Wellness

In the beat of life, emotional health emerges as the foundational pillar that supports a fulfilling and balanced existence. It is within this realm that we shape the contours of our emotional landscapes and fortify our psychological foundations. This chapter shines a spotlight on the profound significance of nurturing our mental health, recognizing that it is not merely a choice but a fundamental necessity for a wholesome life.

Nurturing Resilience

Mental strength equips us with the tools to face life's challenges head-on. It fosters resilience, the ability to bounce back from adversity with strength and determination. When our mental health is robust, we are better prepared to weather the storms of life, adapt to change, and emerge from difficulties with newfound wisdom.

Strengthening Emotional Fortitude

Our toughness is rooted in a state of inner balance. It empowers us to navigate the complex tapestry of feelings and emotions that enrich our lives. By tending to our inner well-being, we acquire heightened insight, which enables a deeper understanding of ourselves and those around us. This strength facilitates healthier connections and a more enriching social life.

Elevating Overall Quality of Life

Our mental state isn't separate from our holistic health; it's woven into the fabric of our overall well-being. When we place importance on our mental faculties, we bolster our cognitive capacities, sharpen our decision-making prowess, and foster imaginative thought. As a result, the quality of our lives ascends, allowing us to chase our interests, attain our aspirations, and relish the wonders of existence.

A Necessity, Not a Luxury

It's essential to emphasize that nurturing our mental health is not a luxury reserved for a fortunate few but a vital need for all. Investing in our inner well-being is akin to nourishing the roots of a tree, ensuring the strength and vitality of every branch and leaf. The mantra of "I Don't Care" becomes a key to unlocking the path to inner balance, signifying our commitment to what truly matters, ultimately leading to a more satisfying and harmonious life.

In essence, our inner equilibrium acts as a guiding compass, directing us toward a life characterized by resilience, fortitude, and an enhanced quality of existence. It is a fundamental requirement, and this message serves as a potent tool for nurturing our inner harmony.

2

The Burden of Overcaring

"All we have to decide is what to do with the time that is given us."
– Gandalf, The Fellowship of the Ring

Unpacking the Side Effects: How It Impacts Your Well-being

Ever felt stretched too thin, always giving, and rarely receiving? Let's uncover the deeper ripples caused by spreading yourself too thin:

1. Burnout Central:

Imagine running non-stop on a treadmill set to the highest speed – that's overcaring for you. Leading directly to burnout, it leaves you exhausted, with little left for yourself. It's not just about being tired; it's about losing the spark that drives you.

2. Skipping the Self-love:

When you're always on call for others, your own recharge moments — from a peaceful meditation session to that cherished bubble bath — take a back seat. Neglecting self-care means neglecting the foundation of your well-being.

3. Blurred Lines:

Picture your personal boundaries as walls of a fortress. This burden weakens those walls, allowing others to flood in, making it challenging to distinguish where your needs end and theirs begin.

4. Brewing the Resentment Tea:

Like a pot left on the stove for too long, consistently placing others first can cause negative emotions to bubble up, turning your inner world bitter.

5. Chasing External Validation:

If you're continually looking for applause from others, it's like basing your self-worth on shifting sands. It's unstable, unreliable, and can leave you feeling lost in the crowd.

6. Anxiety Overdrive:

Too much care is like having too many apps open on your phone; it drains your battery and slows your performance. The ever-present concern about pleasing everyone turns day-to-day life into a stress fest.

7. Who Am I, Again?:

It's like playing a role for so long that you forget your original character. Immersing yourself too much in others' stories can make you lose sight of your own plotline.

8. The Help Paradox:

Imagine a lifeguard who's always swimming, never resting. Over time, they'll lack the strength to save anyone. When you're constantly drained, your ability to genuinely uplift others diminishes.

9. Joy Deficit:

Life isn't just about making it through the day; it's about thriving. Overcaring, with its exhaustive demands, can cast a shadow over the joys and passions that make life worth living.

So, while being there for others is a gift, remember to save some of that love and energy for yourself. Finding equilibrium (have you seen that movie? Amazing!) between self-love and caring for others is where true harmony and fulfillment reside.

Identifying Stressors Caused by Caring About the Unimportant

Recognizing the sources of stress that arise from caring about unimportant matters is a vital step toward achieving a healthier and more balanced approach to life. Here, we peek into the various stressors associated with expending energy on things that ultimately hold little significance:

1. **Time Wastage**: Caring excessively about unimportant details often results in a significant waste of time. This can include obsessing over minor decisions, perfectionism in inconsequential tasks, and overanalyzing insignificant matters. Such time wastage can lead to increased stress due to a lack of productivity and missed opportunities to

focus on more meaningful pursuits.

2. **Perfectionism**: The pursuit of perfection in unimportant areas can be a major stressor. Perfectionism not only sets unrealistic standards but also places immense pressure on individuals to achieve flawless results, even in situations where excellence is unnecessary.

3. **Decision Fatigue**: Constantly fretting over trivial choices and matters can lead to decision fatigue. When individuals expend mental energy on numerous inconsequential decisions, they may find themselves mentally exhausted when facing more critical choices, which can significantly contribute to stress.

4. **Comparison and Social Pressure**: Caring excessively about unimportant matters can result from societal pressure and the urge to conform to perceived norms. The stressors here involve comparing oneself to others, feeling inadequate due to societal expectations, and attempting to meet arbitrary standards set by society.

5. **Financial Strain**: Overvaluing material possessions and acquiring unnecessary items can lead to financial stress. This form of caring can result in debt, overspending, and financial insecurity, causing significant anxiety and strain.

6. **Conflict and Relationships**: Over-concern about minor disagreements and conflicts can strain relationships. When individuals invest excessive emotional energy in insignificant disputes, it can lead to tension and harm relationships with family, friends, and colleagues.

7. **Health Implications**: Stressors caused by caring about unimportant matters can have adverse effects on physical health. Chronic stress can lead to various health issues, including cardiovascular problems, compromised immune

function, and mental health disorders like anxiety and depression.

8. **Energy Drain**: Focusing on unimportant matters saps mental and emotional energy that could be better invested in more meaningful pursuits. This constant energy drain can result in feelings of exhaustion and frustration.

9. **Reduced Focus on Meaningful Goals**: Over-caring about trivial matters can divert attention away from important life goals and aspirations. This loss of focus on what truly matters can lead to a lack of fulfillment and stress.

By identifying these stressors, individuals can become more aware of the negative impact of caring about the unimportant. This awareness is a crucial first step toward reevaluating priorities, reducing stress, and achieving a more balanced and fulfilling life.

Recognizing the Need for Change

From stretching ourselves thin to finding equilibrium can be truly enlightening; let's dive into the heart of this transformation and uncover the signals that it's time to re-calibrate our psyche:

1. **Awareness**: The first step in recognizing the need for change is becoming aware of the tendency to care too much. This involves introspection and self-reflection to identify instances where caring excessively has led to stress, anxiety, or negative outcomes. It's about acknowledging the impact on mental well-being.

2. **Understanding the Consequences**: Over-caring often

leads to negative consequences such as burnout, heightened stress levels, and strained relationships. Recognizing these consequences is essential in realizing that the current point of view may not be sustainable or healthy in the long run.

3. **Assessing Priorities**: Individuals need to assess their priorities and values. Recognizing the need for change involves asking questions like, "Am I investing too much emotional energy in things that don't truly matter?" or "Is my constant concern for trivial matters affecting my overall happiness?"

4. **Impact on Mental Health**: It's crucial to acknowledge the impact on mental health. Recognizing signs of anxiety, sleep disturbances, or emotional exhaustion can serve as a wake-up call that prompts the desire for change.

5. **Desire for Emotional Well-being**: The recognition of the need for change often arises from a deep desire for emotional well-being and a more relaxed, contented state of mind. Individuals may realize that letting go of unnecessary worries and stressors is essential for their mental health.

6. **Shifting Focus to What Matters**: This recognition involves understanding that constantly caring about trivial matters takes away energy and attention from what truly matters in life. It's about wanting to redirect focus and emotional resources toward meaningful goals and relationships.

7. **Embracing Healthy Detachment**: Recognizing the need for change means acknowledging the value of healthy detachment. It involves understanding that caring too much about every little detail can be draining and counterproductive. Embracing the idea of not caring about things

that are beyond one's control becomes appealing.

8. **Exploring Mindset Shift Strategies**: Once the need for change is recognized, individuals may begin exploring strategies and techniques to shift their mentality. This could involve mindfulness practices, setting boundaries, or seeking support from therapy or self-help resources.

9. **Acceptance of Imperfection**: Part of recognizing the need for change involves accepting one's imperfections and limitations. It's acknowledging that it's okay not to have control over everything and that perfection is an unrealistic standard.

10. **Commitment to Personal Growth**: Ultimately, recognizing the need for a mentality shift to not caring is a commitment to personal growth and well-being. It signifies a willingness to plunge into the world of self-discovery and positive change.

Moving from a heightened level of care to balanced care is about awakening, understanding, re-calibrating, and committing. It's a rich tapestry of self-awareness, forging healthier habits, and dedicating oneself to a brighter, more balanced tomorrow.

3

Unravel: The LOLs and Woes of Overcaring

You've got mail! And it's an invitation to the party of "The Overcarers." If you've RSVPed "Yes," then let's take a wild, enlightening ride through the highs and lows of caring way too much.

Burnout Central:

- *The Treadmill Saga*: Ever felt like a hamster on a wheel? That's overcaring, my friend. Spoiler alert: There's no gold medal for running yourself ragged.

Skipping the Self-love:

- *Bye-Bye Bubble Baths*: When the world dials your number non-stop, that dreamy self-pampering feels like a fairy tale. Remember: Cinderella took her night off!

Blurred Lines:

- *Fortress No More*: If your emotional walls were a castle, overcaring might be the sneaky dragon melting them away.

Brewing the Resentment Tea:

- *Kettle's Screaming*: If resentment were a beverage, overcarers might just be brewing a giant pot. Best served cold? Nah, let's not serve it at all.

Chasing External Validation:

- *Where's My Applause?*: Always in the audience, never the star? Be wary of seeking only outside reviews; sometimes, the inner critic has the best advice.

Anxiety Overdrive:

- *Phone's Dying, and So Am I*: Overcaring = too many mental apps open. You're not the latest model; updates required.

Who Am I, Again?:

- *Lost in the Role*: Played a part so long that your script got lost? Time for a script flip!

The Help Paradox:

- *Tired Lifeguard Tales*: Lifeguards need breaks too. Can't save others if you're gasping for air.

Joy Deficit:

- *Where's the Party?*: When life feels more like surviving than celebrating, I bet you can guess who might be crashing the party.

Stressing Over the Small Stuff:

- *Is that ant REALLY important?*: From wasted time on minutiae to decision fatigue from choosing the *perfect* pen color. Overcaring about trivialities might just be the quickest way to miss the forest for the trees.

In a nutshell? Being there for others is beautiful, but let's not forget the person in the mirror. It's time to find the sweet spot between caring for others and cherishing oneself. Because balance, dear reader, is where the real party's at! (Unlike what Jagged Edge said)

4

Defining Your Priorities

Bring back life form. Priority One. All other priorities rescinded.
– Ash, Alien

Self-Reflection: What Truly Matters to You?

In the hustle and bustle of everyday life, it's easy to get swept away by external demands and distractions. We often find ourselves juggling numerous tasks, meeting deadlines, and trying to please others. But amidst this chaos, have you ever paused to ask yourself, **"What truly matters to me?"**

Self-reflection is the compass that guides us on our path to defining our priorities. It's the process of looking inward, peeling back the layers of societal expectations and external pressures, to uncover the core values and desires that reside within us.

Why Self-Reflection Matters:

1. **Clarity**: Self-reflection brings clarity to your life. It allows

you to sift through the noise and identify what holds genuine significance to you. It's like polishing a foggy mirror to reveal a crystal-clear reflection of your true desires.

2. **Alignment**: When you understand what truly matters, you can align your actions and choices with your values. This alignment leads to a sense of purpose and fulfillment.

3. **Reduced Stress**: Knowing your priorities helps you set boundaries and say no to things that don't align with them. This reduces stress and prevents you from spreading yourself too thin.

4. **Improved Decision-Making**: Self-reflection enhances your decision-making abilities. When you're clear about your priorities, making choices becomes easier because you can evaluate options based on what matters most to you.

How to Begin Self-Reflection:

1. **Create Quiet Space**: Find a quiet, comfortable space where you won't be disturbed. It could be a cozy corner in your home, a park bench, or a quiet room. Silence the external noise to hear your inner voice.

2. **Set Aside Time**: Dedicate specific time for self-reflection. It could be a few minutes each day or a longer session once a week. Consistency is key.

3. **Ask Questions**: Start by asking yourself probing questions. What are your core values? What brings you joy and fulfillment? What are your long-term aspirations? What are you willing to let go of to make room for what matters?

4. **Journaling**: Consider keeping a journal to document your

thoughts and insights during self-reflection. Writing can be a powerful tool for self-discovery.

5. **Meditation and/or Mindfulness**: Practices like these can help you become more attuned to your inner self. They encourage stillness and introspection.
6. **Seek Feedback**: Sometimes, feedback from trusted friends or a therapist can provide valuable insights into your priorities. They may see aspects of you that you haven't fully recognized.

Remember, self-reflection is an ongoing process. It's not about finding all the answers immediately but about gradually uncovering what truly matters to you. As we trudge on, we'll burrow deeper into the art of self-reflection and explore how it plays a pivotal role in defining your priorities.

The Value of Prioritization

Now that we've engaged in self-reflection and pinpointed what holds significance for you, it's time to rummage through the profound influence of prioritizing on your overall state of well-being. Prioritization extends beyond being a mere time management technique; it stands as a fundamental principle capable of shaping the quality of your life and your holistic health.

Why Prioritization Matters:

1. **Reduced Overwhelm**: When you prioritize, you focus your energy on the most important aspects of your life. This reduces the sense of overwhelm that often accompanies

trying to manage everything at once.

2. **Enhanced Clarity**: Prioritization brings clarity to your goals and aspirations. It helps you distinguish between what's urgent and what's truly important. This clarity empowers you to make purposeful choices.

3. **Stress Reduction**: By identifying your priorities, you create a roadmap for your life. This roadmap minimizes stress by allowing you to allocate your time and resources efficiently.

4. **Improved Decision-Making**: Prioritization sharpens your decision-making skills. When faced with choices, you can evaluate them based on how well they align with your priorities.

5. **Increased Fulfillment**: When you focus on what truly matters to you, you derive a deeper sense of fulfillment and purpose from your actions and accomplishments.

Steps to Effective Prioritization:

1. **Rank Your Priorities**: Take the time to rank your priorities. What comes first, second, and third? This ranking will guide your decision-making process.

2. **Set Clear Goals**: Define clear and specific goals related to your priorities. These goals act as milestones, helping you track your progress.

3. **Time Allocation**: Allocate your time and resources in alignment with your priorities. Ensure that your daily activities reflect your values.

4. **Learn to Say No**: Saying no to activities or commitments that don't align with your priorities is a powerful skill. It creates space for what truly matters.

5. **Review and Adjust**: Regularly review your priorities and

assess if they still resonate with you. Life evolves, and your priorities may shift accordingly.

6. **Seek Support**: Share your priorities with loved ones or a support network. They can provide encouragement and help you stay accountable.

As we continue our exploration, remember that this trek is a dynamic one. Prioritization is not a one-time task but a continuous process that evolves as you grow and change. By learning to do this effectively, you take significant steps toward achieving balance, happiness, and well-being in your life.

Setting Clear Personal Goals and Values

We've established the importance of prioritization. Let's delve deeper into the process of setting clear personal goals and values. This step is integral to aligning your actions with what truly matters to you.

The Role of Personal Goals and Values:

1. **Guiding Principles**: Personal values are the core principles that define who you are and what you stand for. They serve as your moral compass, guiding your decisions and actions.
2. **Goals as Milestones**: Personal goals are tangible, actionable steps that you take to manifest your values. They act as milestones towards living a purposeful life.

How to Set Clear Personal Goals and Values:

1. **Self-Reflection**: Begin by reflecting on your values. What

principles are most important to you? Common values include integrity, compassion, family, and personal growth. Take time to identify and prioritize them.

2. **Define Your Aspirations**: What do you want to achieve in various aspects of your life? Whether it's in your career, relationships, or personal development, define clear aspirations that align with your values.

3. **SMART Goals**: Use the SMART (Specific, Measurable, Achievable, Relevant, Time-bound) criteria to frame your goals. This ensures that your goals are well-defined and actionable.

4. **Break It Down**: Divide larger goals into smaller, manageable steps. This makes your goals less daunting and more achievable.

5. **Write Them Down**: Putting your goals and values in writing solidifies your commitment to them. Keep a journal or create a vision board to visualize your aspirations.

6. **Seek Alignment**: Ensure that your goals align with your values. If a goal contradicts a core value, it may lead to inner conflict and dissatisfaction.

7. **Regular Review**: Periodically review your goals and values. Are they still relevant? Have they changed over time? Adjust them as needed.

Benefits of Setting Clear Goals and Values:

1. **Purposeful Living**: Clarity in your values and goals allows you to live with purpose. You have a clear direction and motivation.

2. **Enhanced Decision-Making**: When faced with choices, you can evaluate them based on whether they align with

your values and goals, making decision-making more straightforward.

3. **Fulfillment**: Achieving goals that resonate with your values brings a deep sense of fulfillment and satisfaction.
4. **Reduced Stress**: Clear goals reduce uncertainty and stress. You know where you're heading and how to get there.
5. **Improved Well-Being**: Living in alignment with your values and pursuing meaningful goals contributes to overall well-being and mental health.

Remember that your values and goals are exclusive to you. They reflect your authentic self. By setting clear personal goals and values, you lay the foundation for a purpose-driven life that promotes emotional stability and fulfillment.

5

Unravel: Finding the 'You' in 'Busy'

Alright, buckle up, fellow traveler. In the mad rush of life (think juggling flaming torches while riding a unicycle), you ever stop and ponder, "Hey, what the heck am I doing all this for?" If not, fear not! Chapter 4 was here to hand you a mirror, a compass, and maybe a snack. (Okay, no snack, but the metaphorical goodies are pretty good too!)

Introspection 101: "Mirror, Mirror on the Wall": What matters to YOU? Not your dog, not the mailman, YOU! This isn't just about finding out if you prefer latte over cappuccino. It's about clarity, alignment, stress reduction, and smarter decision-making. And yes, that involves some 'me-time,' writing in a diary, meditation, and perhaps a heart-to-heart with trusted friends (or a professional).

The Big "P": Prioritization: Ahoy! Overwhelm ahoy! We're diving deep into the ocean of prioritization, where we'll discover that it's not about catching every fish but just the ones that make your heart sing (and stomach satisfied, if we're still talking fish).

From setting boundaries to acing decisions, prioritization is your magic wand. Wave goodbye to stress and say hello to a purpose-driven life!

Goals and Values - Your GPS and Compass: Remember that time you got lost in the supermarket? Goals and values are your personal GPS and compass for life. They give direction, purpose, and a sense of "I've got this!" Whether it's career goals, personal values, or deciding if you should get that extra scoop of ice cream - having them clear makes everything easier and a lot more fun.

Chapter 4 was all about pausing, pondering, and powering through with purpose. And remember, in the grand circus of life, it's not about how many balls you can juggle, but which ones deserve your time and attention. Go forth and ! And maybe grab a snack after all.

6

Letting Go of the Unimportant

"Stop trying to control everything and just let go. Let go!"
- Tyler Durden, Fight Club

Strategies to Identify Unimportant Things in Life

In our pursuit of a fulfilling life, one of the most crucial steps is learning to let go of the unimportant. Often, we are weighed down by unnecessary clutter in our minds and lifestyles, preventing us from focusing on what truly matters. Luckily, there are effective strategies to identify and tidy up the unimportant aspects of your life:

1. Self-Reflection and Prioritization:
Begin by taking a step back and reflecting on your life's priorities. What truly matters to you? What are your long-term goals and values? Identifying your core values and goals will provide a solid foundation for recognizing what is unimportant in comparison.

2. The 80/20 Rule (Pareto Principle):

The 80/20 rule suggests that 80% of results come from 20% of efforts. Apply this principle to your life – assess which activities, relationships, or commitments contribute the most to your well-being and happiness. Focus your time and energy on these vital few, and consider letting go of the trivial many.

3. Declutter Your Physical Space:

Physical clutter often mirrors mental clutter. Start by purging your physical environment. Identify possessions, objects, or items that no longer serve a purpose or bring joy to your life. Donate, sell, or discard them to create a cleaner and more organized space.

4. Audit Your Commitments:

Review your current commitments, whether they are work-related, social, or personal. Are there obligations that no longer align with your priorities or values? It might be time to gracefully step away from commitments that no longer contribute positively to your life.

5. Practice Mindfulness:

Mindfulness allows you to be fully present and aware of your thoughts, feelings, and experiences. By practicing mindfulness, you can become more attuned to the activities or thoughts that drain your energy without providing significant benefits.

6. Seek Feedback:

Sometimes, we may not see the unimportant aspects of our lives clearly. Seek feedback from trusted friends, family members, or mentors who can provide an objective perspective on where you might be overcommitting or investing energy in unimportant matters.

7. Keep a Journal:
Maintaining a journal can be an effective way to track your daily activities, thoughts, and emotions. Over time, this record can help you identify patterns and areas where you may be spending excessive time and energy on unimportant matters.

By implementing these strategies, you'll begin to develop a keen awareness of the unimportant elements in your life. This newfound clarity will pave the way for greater focus on what truly matters, leading you toward an improved and more purposeful existence.

Techniques for Detaching Emotionally from the Unimportant

Identifying the unimportant aspects of your life is only the first step. To truly let go and target what matters, you must also learn to detach emotionally from the unimportant. Emotions often tie us to things, people, or activities that no longer serve us. This section analyzes techniques to do just that:

1. Practice Mindfulness Meditation:
Mindfulness meditation is a powerful tool for becoming aware of your emotions and learning to observe them without judgment. Regular meditation sessions can help you recognize when you're becoming emotionally entangled with unimportant matters and give you the tools to let go.

2. Accept Imperfection:

Many times, we emotionally invest in perfectionism, striving for flawless outcomes in trivial matters. Embrace the idea that perfection is unattainable in all aspects of life. By accepting imperfection, you can detach from that need for everything to be just right.

3. Set Boundaries:

Establish clear boundaries in your relationships and commitments. Learning to say no when necessary can prevent you from overextending yourself in areas that are not important to your well-being.

4. Shift Your Focus:

When you find yourself becoming emotionally attached to something unimportant, consciously shift your focus to what truly matters. Remind yourself of your core values and priorities to redirect your energy.

5. Create a "Letting Go" Ritual:

Develop a personal ritual that symbolizes your willingness to release emotional attachments to unimportant things. This could involve writing down what you're letting go of and physically discarding it, signifying your commitment to putting what matters most, first.

6. Practice Gratitude:

Cultivating a sense of gratitude for what you have and what truly matters in your life can help you detach from what doesn't. Regularly reflecting on the things you're grateful for can shift your emotional focus.

7. Seek Support:

Sometimes, it's challenging to detach on your own. Reach out to a therapist, counselor, or support group to discuss your attachments and gain insights into how to let go.

8. Visualize Your Ideal Life:

Create a mental image of your ideal life, where you've arranged what truly matters. Visualization can help you emotionally detach from what's unimportant by giving you a clear picture of your desired future.

By practicing these techniques, you'll develop the grit needed to let go of the unimportant. Embracing this detachment is a pivotal step toward achieving your ideal life.

Practical Exercises to Straighten Out Your Mental Space

Focusing on what truly matters in mental health involves not only understanding the concepts but also actively organizing your mental space. This chapter provides a set of practical exercises designed to help you clear the mental clutter and focus on what's important:

1. Mindful Note-Taking:

Begin a practice where you record your thoughts, feelings, and daily experiences. Through regular recording, you can identify patterns of over-caring and discover areas where you need to let go. Reflect on how these thoughts and feelings align with your priorities.

2. The "Two-List" Exercise:

Create two lists: one for what truly matters to you and another for the things that don't. Compare these lists regularly and take action to eliminate or reduce the time and energy you invest in the unimportant list.

3. Digital Detox:

Spend a day or weekend away from digital devices and social media. Use this time to reconnect with yourself and your surroundings, gaining clarity on what digital distractions consume your mental space unnecessarily.

4. The "One-Month Challenge":

Choose one aspect of your life where you tend to over-care about the unimportant. Commit to a one-month challenge of reducing your emotional investment in this area. Track your progress and observe how it affects your mental state.

5. Meditative Practices:

Explore meditative techniques like body scans, progressive muscle relaxation, or loving-kindness meditation. These practices can help you become more aware of the physical and emotional tension associated with over-caring, allowing you to release it.

6. Daily Prioritization Ritual:

Start each day with a prioritization ritual. Identify the key tasks or aspects of your life that align with what truly matters. Make a conscious decision to invest your time and energy in these areas while minimizing distractions and over-caring.

7. The "Gratitude Challenge":

Create a gratitude journal where you write down three things you're grateful for every day. This exercise helps shift your focus toward the constructive aspects of life and reinforces what truly matters.

8. Emotional Detoxification:

Regularly assess your emotional well-being. If you find yourself carrying excess baggage from past events or relationships, seek therapy or counseling to help you release and process these emotions.

9. Visualization for Mental Clarity:

Dedicate time for visualization exercises where you picture a clutter-free mental space. Visualize yourself letting go of unnecessary thoughts and emotions, creating room for what truly matters.

These practical exercises are tools to help you actively clean up your mental space and create room for what's important in your life. By engaging in these activities regularly, you'll strengthen your ability to prioritize and experience mental clarity. Remember that this is about progress, not perfection, and each exercise brings you closer to a more fulfilling life.

7

Unravel: Why Keep the Fluff When You Can Have the Stuff?

Ever feel like your brain's filled with too much... *fluff*? Let's talk decluttering: not your garage, but your *life*. Here's how to ditch the excess baggage and focus on the real deal:

1. **Self-Reflective Soul-Searching:** Dive deep into your soul's wish list. If it doesn't make the cut, chuck it!
2. **80/20 Magic Rule:** Surprise! Only 20% of what you do actually matters. Time to play favorites and ditch the rest.
3. **Tidy Spaces, Tidy Mind:** Got stuff you don't need? Donate, sell, or – if it's that ugly vase from Aunt Gertrude – secretly trash it.
4. **Commitment Audit:** If it doesn't spark joy or align with your Master Life Plan™, say "Thank U, Next!" to those commitments.
5. **Mindfulness Mojo:** Be in the now. If it's draining your vibes, you know the drill – let it go!
6. **Feedback Fiesta:** Ask buddies what they think. They might see the fluff you missed!

7. **Dear Diary:** Jot down your daily dramas. You might just find patterns in your personal soap opera.

Emotionally stuck to the stuff that's not the *real* stuff? Try these:

1. **Meditation Magic:** Tune in to let go!
2. **Embrace Imperfections:** Life's not a Pinterest board. Sometimes, it's okay to be a bit... wonky.
3. **Boundary Bootcamp:** Sometimes, saying no is saying yes to YOU!
4. **Eye on the Prize:** When in doubt, zoom out. Remember the big picture!
5. **Bye-Bye Ritual:** Write. Burn. Release. Repeat.
6. **Attitude of Gratitude:** Flip the script and focus on the good stuff.
7. **Team Therapy:** Sometimes, we all need a little chat (or a lot).
8. **Life in HD:** Visualize a fluff-free future.

And for the overachievers, here's a decathlon of exercises:

1. **Thought Tracker:** Journal it out.
2. **List Love:** Must-haves vs. Meh.
3. **Digital Detox Daze:** Unplug and unwind.
4. **Feng Shui Fun Day:** Less mess, less stress.
5. **One-Month Wonder:** Focus on one fluff, and fling it!
6. **Meditation Mashup:** From body scans to good vibes, find your zen.
7. **Daily Mission:** What's on today's highlight reel?
8. **Thankful Threes:** Daily trio of joys.
9. **Emo Evacuation:** Shed those old emotional cobwebs.

10. **Mental Movie Time:** Visualize the VIP version of you.

In summary, life's short. Why crowd it with the fluff when you can have the *real* stuff?

8

The Power of Saying "No"

"You cannot live your life to please others. The choice must be
yours."
– White Queen, Alice in Wonderland

The Art of Graceful Refusal

In a world filled with endless demands, commitments, and obligations, the power of saying no is a transformative skill. This chapter explores the art of saying no and its profound impact on your mental well-being.

The Weight of Yes

Saying yes to every request or invitation, whether from friends, family, or colleagues, can lead to over commitment and overwhelm. It's essential to recognize that every yes carries a weight, both in terms of time and energy. When we consistently say yes to things that don't align with our priorities, we risk neglecting what truly matters.

The Liberation of No

Contrary to popular belief, saying no is not selfish or unkind; it's an act of self-love and boundary-setting. Learning to say no allows you to:

1. **Protect Your Mental Space**: By saying no to unnecessary commitments, you create space for the things that genuinely matter to you. This protective boundary ensures your mental well-being remains a priority.

2. **Maintain Your Priorities**: Saying no enables you to stay focused on your goals and values. It prevents the dilution of your time and energy on activities that don't contribute to your personal growth and happiness.

3. **Reduce Stress and Overwhelm**: Over-committing can lead to stress and burnout. Saying no helps you manage your workload and commitments, reducing the risk of mental exhaustion.

4. **Enhance Self-Respect**: Setting boundaries through saying "no" communicates self-respect. It signals that you value your time and well-being, which can impact your self-esteem, in a good way.

The Mastery of Declining

Saying no effectively is an art that requires practice and finesse. We will look at practical strategies and techniques to help you master this essential skill. You'll learn how to say no gracefully, assertively, and without guilt, empowering you to reclaim control over your mental space.

The Craft of Standing Firm

Assertiveness is a crucial component of mastering the art of saying no. It empowers you to communicate your boundaries and preferences clearly and respectfully. Let's look at the principles of assertiveness and how they can help you navigate various situations where saying no is necessary.

The Three Communication Styles

1. **Passive**: A passive communication style often involves avoiding conflict at all costs. People with a passive communication style may find it challenging to say no, leading to feelings of frustration and powerlessness. They may agree to things they don't want to do to avoid confrontation.
2. **Aggressive**: On the other end of the spectrum is an aggressive communication style. This style involves asserting one's needs and desires at the expense of others. Aggressive individuals may say no forcefully, but their approach can be hurtful and damaging to relationships.
3. **Assertive**: The assertive communication style strikes a balance between passivity and aggression. It involves expressing your needs, boundaries, and opinions in a clear and respectful manner. Assertive individuals can say no firmly while considering the feelings and perspectives of others.

The Benefits of Assertiveness

Mastering assertiveness offers several benefits:

1. **Effective Communication**: Assertive communication en-

sures that your message is heard and understood. It promotes healthy dialogue and mutual respect.

2. **Enhanced Relationships**: Assertive individuals often have healthier, more respectful relationships because they can communicate their needs and boundaries effectively.

3. **Reduced Stress**: By confidently expressing your boundaries and saying no when necessary, you reduce the internal conflict and stress associated with people-pleasing.

Building Assertiveness Skills

Developing assertiveness skills is a process that involves self-awareness and practice. Here are some strategies to help you become more assertive:

1. **Introspection/Self-Reflection**: Take time to understand yourself. This means looking at your values, needs, and boundaries. This self-awareness is the foundation of assertive communication.

2. **Use "I" Statements**: When expressing yourself, use "I" statements to convey your feelings and needs without blaming or accusing others.

3. **Practice Active Listening**: Part of assertiveness is listening actively to others. It demonstrates respect and empathy.

4. **Set Boundaries**: Clearly define your personal boundaries and make sure to share them to others when necessary.

5. **Role-Play**: Practice assertive communication in various scenarios to build your confidence.

Keep going. We can look at ways you can develop your assertiveness skills. Mastery of assertive communication will enable you to say no with confidence, protecting your mental well-being and focusing on what truly matters in your life.

Learning to Say "No" Without Guilt

Saying "no" without guilt is a skill that can significantly improve your psychological well-being. Many people struggle with guilt when declining requests or setting boundaries, but it's essential to remember that prioritizing your well-being is not selfish. Believe it or not, there are techniques that empower you to decline confidently, free from undue guilt.

The Guilt Trap

Guilt often arises when we fear disappointing or letting down others. It can stem from a desire to please everyone or avoid conflict. However, excessive guilt can lead to Over-committing, stress, and a lack of focus on what truly matters to you.

Strategies for Guilt-Free Nos

1. **Practice Self-Compassion**: Treat yourself with the same kindness and understanding that you would offer to a friend. Understand that it's okay to focus on your well-being.
2. **Set Clear Boundaries**: Establishing and communicating your boundaries helps others understand your limits. When you say "no," it's a reaffirmation of those boundaries.
3. **Use Empathetic Communication**: When declining a request, express understanding and empathy for the other person's needs while staying true to your own boundaries.
4. **Prioritize Your Needs**: Remember that taking care of

your emotional and mental health is a priority. By saying "no" when necessary, you protect your emotional and psychological health.

5. **Let Go of Perfectionism**: Accept that you cannot be everything to everyone. Embrace imperfection and focus on what truly matters to you.
6. **Practice Self-Affirmation**: Remind yourself of your values and priorities when guilt creeps in. Affirm your commitment to your well-being.

The Liberating Power of "No"

Saying "no" when appropriate liberates you from unnecessary obligations and allows you to channel your energy and time into what aligns with your values. It's a step towards self-empowerment and mental clarity.

Practical exercises and real-life scenarios can help you build your confidence in saying "no" without guilt. As you master this skill, you'll free yourself from the burden of over-committing and cultivate a greater sense of well-being.

Boundary Setting for Mental Well-being

Boundaries are like the guardrails on the highway of your life. They define the limits of what is acceptable and safe for you. Without clear boundaries, you may find yourself constantly overwhelmed, stressed, and unable to focus on your mental well-being.

The Significance of Boundaries

1. **Protect Your Energy**: Boundaries safeguard your emo-

tional and mental energy. They prevent others from draining your resources and ensure that you have the capacity to take care of yourself.

2. **Maintain Clarity**: Clear boundaries provide clarity in relationships and interactions. They help others understand what is acceptable and expected, reducing misunderstandings and conflicts.

3. **Preserve Self-Respect**: Setting and enforcing boundaries is an act of self-respect. It communicates that you value yourself and your well-being.

4. **Enhance Focus**: When you have well-defined boundaries, you can focus your time and energy on what truly matters to you. This reduces distractions and enhances your mental clarity.

Types of Boundaries

1. **Physical Boundaries**: These involve personal space and touch. Physical boundaries ensure your comfort and safety.

2. **Emotional Boundaries**: Emotional boundaries dictate how much of your emotions and feelings you are willing to share with others. They protect you from emotional manipulation.

3. **Time Boundaries**: Time boundaries are about managing your schedule and commitments. They help you allocate time for self-preservation and put your inner peace first.

4. **Material Boundaries**: Material boundaries pertain to your belongings and resources. Setting limits on how your possessions are used can prevent stress and conflicts.

How to Set Boundaries

1. **Self-Awareness**: Reflect on your needs, values, and limits. Understand what is essential for your mental well-being.
2. **Communication**: Clearly and assertively communicate your boundaries to others. Be direct and respectful when expressing your limits.
3. **Consistency**: Enforce your boundaries consistently. People will respect your limits more when they see that you consistently uphold them.
4. **Self-Care**: Set this as a part of your boundaries. Allocate time for activities that rejuvenate your mental health.
5. **Seek Support**: Don't hesitate to seek support from friends, family, or professionals in boundary-setting if needed.

Establishing and maintaining boundaries is a continuous process, and it may take time to become comfortable with this practice. However, as you become adept at setting and enforcing boundaries, you'll find that your mental well-being improves, and you have more control over your life.

9

Unravel: Mastering the 'No' - A Humorous Insight

Ever been crushed by the weight of one too many "yeses"? Chapter 8 dug deep into the jungle of commitments, making you the Indiana Jones of decision-making.

The Weight of Yes

Imagine saying yes to EVERYTHING. "Want to go bungee-jumping off this questionable bridge?" "Yes!" "Fancy joining the 'Underwater Basket Weaving Club'?" "Sure!" Well, saying yes to everything, from grandma's cat party to your boss's weekend PowerPoint Party (yawn), can lead you straight to Burnoutville. Remember, every 'yes' is like adding one more brick to your backpack. How heavy do you want it to be?

The Liberation of No

Breathe in, breathe out, and... say "NO". It's not mean, it's just smart! Benefits include:

1. Keeping your sanity.

2. Not losing sight of your life goals (like binge-watching that new show).
3. Avoiding the dreaded burnout.
4. Boosting your ego because, hey, you're important too!

The Mastery of Declining

Saying no with style! No, it's not a new dance move, but it is an art. Get ready for some tips and tricks to reject with flair!

The Craft of Standing Firm

Ever met someone so passive they might as well be a doormat? Or someone so aggressive you thought they might breathe fire? Aim for the middle with assertiveness. It's like Goldilocks – not too soft, not too hard, just right.

Communication Styles 101

1. Passive: "Oh, alright, I'll do it... again."
2. Aggressive: "NO, and also, NEVER!"
3. Assertive: "No thank you, I've got my plate full with unicorn grooming."

Learning to Say "No" Without Guilt

Guilt after saying no? We've all been there. It's like eating a salad and feeling bad you didn't pick the fries. But fear not! Dive in to master the fine art of guiltless rejection.

Boundary Setting for Mental Well-being

Picture this: your life is a magnificent castle, and boundaries are the moat. Keep out the unwanted, let in the cherished, and most importantly, protect your royal sanity!

Ready to commence on this "no"-venture? Too late, Chapter 8 was all about mastering the delicate art of shaking your head!

44

10

Embracing Minimalism

"Say hello to my little friend!"
– Tony Montana, Scarface

Applying Minimalism in Your Life

Minimalism is a lifestyle philosophy that emphasizes simplicity, intentionality, and the removal of excess clutter, both physical and mental. Ever wonder how you can apply minimalism to your life to reduce stress, enhance mental clarity, and establish priorities? Wonder no more!

The Essence of Minimalism

1. **Simplify Your Environment**: Minimalism starts with tidying up your physical surroundings. By removing unnecessary possessions and organizing your space, you create a sense of order and reduce distractions that can contribute to mental clutter.
2. **Quality Over Quantity**: Minimalism encourages you to

focus on the quality of your possessions and experiences rather than accumulating many of them. This mindset shift can lead to a deeper appreciation for what you have, reducing the desire for more and fostering contentment.

3. **Embrace Mindful Consumption**: Minimalism invites you to be mindful of your consumption habits. Before acquiring something new, consider whether it genuinely adds value to your life. This practice helps you avoid impulse purchases and clutter.

4. **Create Mental Space**: Minimalism isn't limited to physical belongings; it also extends to mental clutter. Learn to let go of unnecessary thoughts, worries, and commitments that overwhelm your mind. By creating mental space, you allow room for creativity, clarity, and inner peace.

Applying Minimalism to Different Areas of Life

1. **Physical Possessions**: Start by trimming down your home. Donate or discard items you no longer use or love. Organize your space to be functional and aesthetically pleasing. Having a tidy, simplified living environment can reduce stress and improve your overall well-being.

2. **Digital Minimalism**: Apply minimalism to your digital life by cleaning out your digital devices. Delete unnecessary files, apps, and emails. Limit screen time and social media usage to reduce information overload and improve focus.

3. **Time Management**: Minimalism extends to how you manage your time. Rank tasks and commitments that align with your values and well-being. Learn to say no to over-commitment and create space for relaxation and self-renewal.

4. **Relationships**: Evaluate your relationships and invest time and energy in those that are meaningful and supportive. Minimalism in relationships means focusing on quality connections rather than spreading yourself thin with numerous acquaintances.

Benefits of Minimalism for Brain Health

1. **Reduced Stress**: A simplified life leads to reduced stress and anxiety. Less clutter and fewer commitments mean fewer sources of overwhelm.
2. **Enhanced Focus**: Minimalism can sharpen your focus by eliminating distractions and allowing you to concentrate on what truly matters.
3. **Improved Well-being**: By prioritizing quality experiences and relationships, minimalism can enhance your overall well-being and satisfaction with life.
4. **Greater Clarity**: Minimalism fosters mental clarity by removing mental and physical clutter, allowing you to think more clearly and make better decisions.

Remember that embracing minimalism is a personal and ongoing process. The goal is not to deprive yourself but to intentionally choose what adds value to your life while letting go of what doesn't.

Reducing Material and Mental Clutter

One of the fundamental principles of minimalism is the reduction of both material and mental clutter. By consciously simplifying your life and letting go of unnecessary baggage, you can create space for mental clarity, improved well-being, and a stronger focus on what truly matters. You may remember this from Chapter 6, but like I mentioned at the beginning...spaghetti noodles.

Unclutter Your Physical Environment

1. **Start Small**: Begin by tackling one area or room at a time. This could be your closet, kitchen, or workspace. By breaking the process into manageable steps, it becomes less overwhelming.
2. **The One-In, One-Out Rule**: Adopt the rule that for every new item you bring into your home, one similar item must be donated or discarded. This keeps your possessions in check and prevents accumulation.
3. **Identify Necessities vs. Luxuries**: Distinguish between items you genuinely need and those that are luxuries or rarely used. Minimalism encourages you to keep what serves a practical purpose and brings you joy.
4. **Quality Over Quantity**: Invest in high-quality items that are built to last, rather than buying disposable or cheap products. This not only reduces waste but also enhances your appreciation for the items you own.

Streamlining Your Digital Life

1. **Digital Declutter**: Extend minimalism to your digital world by organizing your digital files, photos, and emails. Delete duplicates and unnecessary files. Unsubscribe from email lists that no longer interest you.
2. **Mindful Social Media Use**: Limit your time on social media

and curate your feed to include content that adds value to your life. Unfollow accounts that trigger negative emotions or contribute to mindless scrolling.

3. **Reduce App Overload**: Review your smartphone apps and delete those you rarely use. This will not only free up space on your device but also reduce the distractions that apps can bring.

Cleansing Your Mind

1. **Practice Mindfulness**: Incorporate mindfulness techniques into your daily routine. Mindfulness helps you become aware of your thoughts and emotions, allowing you to let go of unproductive or negative thinking patterns.
2. **Diary**: Maintain a journal to express your thoughts and feelings. Writing can be a therapeutic way to process emotions and organize your mind.
3. **Set Clear Priorities**: Determine your core values and priorities. Knowing what truly matters to you helps you focus your mental energy on meaningful pursuits.
4. **Learn to Say No**: Embrace saying no to commitments, tasks, or requests that don't align with your goals or values. This prevents overcommitment and mental exhaustion.

The Benefits

Both in the physical and mental realms, this offers numerous benefits:

- **Reduced Stress**: A simplified and organized environment leads to reduced stress levels.
- **Enhanced Focus**: Fewer distractions and mental clutter

mean improved concentration.

- **Greater Productivity**: A clutter-free space and mind enable you to be more productive.
- **Improved Emotional Well-being**: Letting go of emotional baggage and negative thought patterns can lead to better emotional health.

Achieving Mental Clarity through Minimalistic Practices

Embracing minimalism extends beyond sorting out your physical and digital spaces. It also involves adopting intentional practices to achieve mental clarity and simplicity in your daily life. By simplifying your thought processes and routines, you can experience greater peace of mind and enhanced overall well-being.

Mindful Consumption

1. **Intentional Purchasing**: Apply mindfulness to your shopping habits. Before making a purchase, ask yourself if the item aligns with your values and if it's truly necessary. Avoid impulse buying.
2. **Quality Over Quantity**: Look for quality when acquiring new possessions. Investing in items that are built to last reduces the need for constant replacements and clutter.
3. **Digital Detox**: Regularly disconnect from digital devices. Designate specific times for checking emails and social media, allowing you to regain control over your online presence.

Simplified Routines

1. **Morning Ritual**: Begin your day with a simple and mindful morning routine. This can include meditation, stretching, or journaling to set a good tone for the day.
2. **One Task at a Time**: Avoid multitasking, which can lead to mental clutter and decreased productivity. Focus on completing one task before moving on to the next.
3. **Time Blocking**: Organize your schedule by blocking time for specific activities. This helps you allocate dedicated time to important tasks and prevents overloading your calendar.

Mindful Consumption

1. **Mindful Eating**: Practice mindful eating by savoring each bite and paying attention to the flavors and textures of your food. This not only promotes healthier eating habits but also encourages mindfulness in other areas of life.
2. **Gratitude Practice**: Cultivate gratitude by regularly acknowledging and appreciating the positive aspects of your life. This can be done through a daily gratitude journal or simply taking a moment to reflect.
3. **Meditation and Breathing Exercises**: Incorporate meditation and deep breathing exercises into your routine. These practices promote mental clarity, reduce stress, and enhance overall mindfulness.

Digital Minimalism

1. **App Curation**: Reevaluate the apps on your smartphone

and only keep those that add genuine value to your life. Eliminate apps that contribute to mindless scrolling and distractions.

2. **Unsubscribe and Unfollow**: Continuously assess your digital subscriptions and unfollow or unsubscribe from content that no longer serves your interests or well-being.
3. **Scheduled Screen Time**: Set specific times for checking emails and social media rather than constantly engaging with your devices. This allows you to maintain better control over your digital life.

By incorporating these minimalistic practices into your daily routine, you can gradually simplify your life and achieve mental clarity. The pursuit of simplicity involves intentional choices and a commitment to focusing on what truly matters.

11

Unravel: The "Less is More" Life Guide!

Tired of tripping over your sixth pair of shoes or drowning in the sea of unread emails? Welcome to the world of minimalism! In "Embracing Minimalism", we're about to give your life a Marie Kondo-style shakeup, but with a sprinkle of humor.

Just to possibly save you a search: Marie Kondo is famous for her approach to clutter. If you're interested in seeing her philosophies, go look her up!

Minimalism: The Basics

- *Physical Stuff*: Clear out that garage. If you haven't used it in a year, it's time for it to find a new home.
- *Digital Chaos*: Ever opened your smartphone and felt like you've entered a digital maze? Delete, unsubscribe, and unplug. Yes, even from that meme-sharing group. Well, maybe keep that...
- *Mind Matters*: Less overthinking, more zen. Sounds impossible? We've got tips to get that mind of yours a little less

crowded.

Decluttering for Dummies

- **Tip 1**: Start small. Maybe just that junk drawer that holds everything from expired coupons to mysterious keys.
- **Tip 2**: For every new buy, say goodbye to an oldie. New sneakers in? That's one old pair out. (Your closet just sighed in relief!)
- **Tip 3**: High quality over high quantity. Buy things that last longer than your last diet.

Reorganize That Noggin

- **Writing in a Diary:** It's like therapy, but cheaper. Write down those thoughts, and who knows? You might discover you're the next Shakespeare (or at least a solid meme creator).
- **Mindfulness:** Let's turn down the noise. Deep breath in, and out. See? You're practically a monk now.

Digital Trim Down

- Check your apps. Does anyone really need five different weather apps? The sky can only fall so many times, Chicken Little.
- Unfollow and unsubscribe. If it's not dog videos or dessert recipes, is it even worth it?

In short, the last chapter was about giving your life a detox — cleaning up your spaces, your mind, and even your friendships.

And remember, less truly is more (except when it comes to laughter, always have more of that!)

55

12

Cultivating Mindfulness

"The body cannot live without the mind"
– Morpheus, The Matrix

Understanding Mindfulness and Its Benefits

Mindfulness is a powerful practice that can profoundly impact your mental well-being and overall quality of life. It involves being fully present and aware of the present moment, without judgment. In this chapter, we will explore the concept of mindfulness and its numerous benefits.

What is Mindfulness?

Mindfulness is the art of consciously paying attention to the present moment with an open and non-judgmental mindset. It encourages you to become fully aware of your thoughts, emotions, bodily sensations, and the surrounding environment. This practice involves observing your experiences without trying to change them, and accepting them as they are.

Key Elements of Mindfulness:

1. **Present Moment Awareness**: Mindfulness directs your focus to the here and now. It encourages you to let go of worries about the past or future and instead be fully engaged in the present moment.
2. **Non-Judgment**: Mindfulness promotes an attitude of non-judgment. You acknowledge your thoughts and feelings without labeling them as good or bad. This allows for greater self-compassion and self-acceptance.
3. **Observation**: Mindfulness involves observing your thoughts and emotions from a detached perspective. It's like being the silent observer of your inner experiences, which can lead to a deeper understanding of yourself.

Benefits of Mindfulness:

1. **Lowering Stress**: Mindfulness practice has been shown to reduce stress levels significantly. By staying present and not dwelling on past regrets or future worries, you can find relief from stress.
2. **Better Emotional Control**: Mindfulness helps you become more aware of your emotions and how they manifest in your body. This awareness empowers you to respond to challenging emotions in healthier ways.
3. **Enhanced Concentration and Focus**: Regular mindfulness practice can improve your ability to concentrate and sustain attention. This can boost productivity and cognitive performance.
4. **Increased Resilience**: Mindfulness cultivates this by teaching you to adapt to life's challenges with greater ease. It

encourages a more balanced and calm response to adversity.

5. **Better Relationships**: Being fully present in your interactions with others fosters more meaningful and empathetic relationships. Mindfulness can enhance your ability to listen and communicate effectively.

6. **Improved Sleep**: Many individuals find that mindfulness helps alleviate insomnia and improves the quality of their sleep.

These following practices will empower you to harness the benefits of mindfulness and cultivate a more mindful and mentally healthy existence.

Techniques for Mindful Living

Mindfulness is a skill that can be developed and integrated into various aspects of your life. By incorporating mindfulness techniques into your daily routine, you can enhance your mind and experience greater fulfillment. Here are some practical techniques for mindful living:

1. Mindful Breathing:

- **Deep Breathing**: Take a few minutes each day to practice deep, intentional breathing. Focus your attention on the sensation of your breath as it enters and leaves your body. This simple exercise can help calm your mind and reduce stress.

- **Breath Awareness**: Throughout the day, pause for a moment to pay attention to your breath. Notice its rhythm and how it feels as it moves in and out. This quick mindfulness check-in can bring you back to the present moment.

2. Mindful Eating:

- **Savor Your Food**: When you eat, slow down and savor each bite. Pay attention to the flavors, textures, and smells of your food. Eating mindfully can enhance your appreciation of meals and promote healthier eating habits.
- **No Distractions**: Avoid eating in front of the TV or computer. Instead, sit at a table and focus solely on your meal. This practice encourages mindful eating and better digestion.

3. Mindful Walking:

- **Walking Meditation**: Take mindful walks, especially in nature. As you walk, pay attention to each step, the sensation of your feet touching the ground, and the sounds and sights around you. This can be a soothing and grounding practice.

4. Body Scan:

- **Progressive Relaxation**: Lie down or sit comfortably and slowly scan your body from head to toe. Notice any areas of tension or discomfort and consciously relax those muscles. This practice can release physical tension and promote relaxation.

5. Mindful Capturing:

- **Reflective Writing**: Dedicate a few minutes each day to writing about your thoughts and emotions. This self-reflection can help you gain insight into your mental state and promote self-awareness.

6. Mindful Listening:

- **Active Listening**: When engaging in conversations, practice active listening. Give your full attention to the person speaking, without interrupting or formulating your response in advance. This fosters better communication and connection.

7. Gratitude Practice:

- **Daily Gratitude**: Before bed or in the morning, list three things you're grateful for. This simple practice can shift your focus toward the positive aspects of your life and boost your mood.

8. Mindful Technology Use:

- **Digital Detox**: Take breaks from screens and social media. Set specific times to check your devices and resist the urge to constantly scroll. Mindful technology use can reduce information overload and stress.

Incorporating these techniques into your daily life can help you cultivate mindfulness and experience its numerous benefits. By making mindfulness a habit, you'll be better equipped to manage stress, enhance your emotional well-being, and live a more balanced and fulfilling life.

How Mindfulness Helps You Focus on What Truly Matters

In our fast-paced and often chaotic lives, it's easy to become overwhelmed by a never-ending stream of tasks, distractions, and external pressures. This constant busyness can lead to a sense of disconnection from what truly matters to us. However, mindfulness offers a powerful antidote to this modern dilemma.

Present-Moment Awareness

Mindfulness is fundamentally about being fully present in the moment. When you practice mindfulness, you bring your attention to the here and now, letting go of regrets about the past and worries about the future. By doing so, you create a mental space where you can connect with your inner self and gain clarity about your priorities.

Reduced Reactivity

One of the key benefits of mindfulness is reduced reactivity to stressors and emotional triggers. Instead of reacting impulsively to challenging situations, you learn to respond thoughtfully. This increased tenacity allows you to make choices aligned with your values rather than reacting to external pressures.

Enhanced Self-Awareness

Mindfulness cultivates self-awareness by encouraging you to observe your thoughts, feelings, and bodily sensations without judgment. Through this self-reflection, you gain insight into your desires, values, and aspirations. You can identify what truly matters to you on a deep, personal level.

Clarification of Priorities

With self-awareness comes the ability to clarify your priorities. Mindfulness helps you distinguish between the essential and the trivial. It allows you to recognize what brings you fulfillment and purpose, enabling you to make intentional choices aligned with your values.

Improved Decision-Making

Mindfulness enhances your cognitive abilities, including decision-making. By staying present and reducing cognitive clutter, you can make clearer, more rational choices that reflect your true priorities.

Deeper Relationships

Mindfulness not only improves your relationship with yourself but also with others. By being fully present in your interactions, you can forge deeper connections and understand the needs and values of those around you.

Reduced Distraction

In a world filled with constant distractions, mindfulness helps you regain control over your attention. By focusing on the present moment, you can minimize the pull of irrelevant or unimportant matters, allowing you to channel your energy into what truly matters.

Stress Reduction

Finally, mindfulness is a potent stress-reduction tool. When you learn to manage stress through mindfulness practices, you free up mental space and emotional energy to concentrate on your priorities.

In this chapter, we explored how mindfulness can be applied in various aspects of your life, helping you connect with what truly matters and guiding you toward a more intentional and fulfilling existence. I try to always be aware of the present moment; it's nice!

13

Unravel: Mindfully Not Losing Your Zen in the 21st Century

Welcome to the world of mindfulness - where being 'in the moment' isn't just for Instagram captions! Let's work on becoming more present, less judgmental, and maybe, just maybe, not flip the table when the Wi-Fi stops working.

Mindfulness 101: Imagine being at a party, and instead of being that guy lost in past regrets or future "what-ifs," you're the cool, calm, collected one enjoying the dip and chatting about the weather. That's mindfulness. You're in the now, and the now is fabulous (especially with that dip).

The Ingredients for Cooking Up Mindfulness:

- **Present Moment Awareness**: Say goodbye to dwelling on that awkward thing you said 5 years ago.
- **Non-Judgment**: Think of it as Marie Kondo-ing your thoughts. Does this judgment spark joy? No? Thank it and let it go.

- **Observation**: Become the Sherlock Holmes of your own mind. Observe, don't judge.

Why Bother with Mindfulness?

1. Stress who? You're too present for that.
2. Become the emotional ninja you were born to be.
3. Get that laser focus without even needing lasers.
4. Channel your inner rubber band – resilient and ready to bounce back!
5. Build relationships stronger than your Wi-Fi connection.
6. Say 'night night' to insomnia.

Practical Ways to Level Up Your Mindfulness Game:

- Breathe like you mean it.
- Eat like it's your first date.
- Walk like you're on the runway.
- Scan your body like you forgot where you placed your keys.
- Write in your journal like you're pen pals with your soul.
- Listen like you're in a suspense movie.
- Show gratitude like it's going out of style.
- Use tech mindfully, like a hipster with a typewriter.

Finally, in the wise words of a forgotten sage (or maybe just me): if you're tired of the chaos, let mindfulness be your GPS back to what truly matters. Hopefully, you learned how to steer your ship (or yoga mat) towards a more intentional life. Namaste!

14

Strategies for Handling External Pressure

"Napoleon, Give Me Some Of Your Tots."
- Randy, Napoleon Dynamite

Navigating Social Expectations

In our interconnected society, we often find ourselves subjected to a multitude of social expectations. These expectations can come from family, friends, colleagues, and even society at large. While some social expectations are reasonable and aligned with our values, others may be burdensome and contribute to stress and anxiety.

Recognizing the Influence of Social Expectations

To effectively navigate social expectations, it's essential to recognize their impact on our lives. These expectations can encompass various aspects, such as career choices, relationships, lifestyle, and even appearance. They often stem from cultural norms, peer pressure, or societal trends.

The Struggle Between Conformity and Authenticity

Navigating social expectations can lead to an internal struggle between conformity and authenticity. We may feel torn between conforming to societal norms and staying true to our genuine desires and values. This conflict can create stress and inner turmoil.

The Need for Assertiveness

One key strategy for handling external pressure from social expectations is assertiveness. Assertiveness involves communicating our needs, preferences, and boundaries respectfully and confidently. It allows us to assert our values and priorities without being overly influenced by external pressures.

Setting Personal Boundaries

Establishing clear personal boundaries is another crucial aspect of managing social expectations. Boundaries help define what you are comfortable with and what you are not. They enable you to protect your mental well-being by preventing others from imposing their expectations upon you.

Prioritizing Your Values

To navigate social expectations effectively, it's important to give precedence to your values. By identifying what truly matters to you, you can make decisions that align with your authentic self. This empowers you to resist the pressure to conform to expectations that don't resonate with your values.

Open Communication

Open and honest communication with those who impose expectations on you is key. Express your thoughts, feelings, and boundaries clearly to help others understand your perspective. This can lead to more supportive and understanding relationships.

Self-Reflection

Self-reflection is a powerful tool for evaluating the social expectations you face. Take time to assess whether these expectations are in harmony with your values and goals. This introspective process allows you to differentiate between meaningful aspirations and external pressures.

Mindful Decision-Making

As discussed in previous chapters, mindfulness can be instrumental in handling external pressure. By staying present and mindful in decision-making, you can make choices that align with your values and minimize the influence of external expectations.

Dealing with Peer Pressure and Comparison

Peer pressure and the tendency to compare ourselves to others are common sources of external pressure that can significantly impact our mental well-being. Whether in social circles, at work, or in the age of social media, the pressure to conform or measure up to others' standards can be overwhelming.

Understanding Peer Pressure

Peer pressure refers to the influence that our peers, friends, or colleagues exert on us to conform to their beliefs, behaviors, or expectations. It can manifest in various forms, from subtle suggestions to more explicit demands. Peer pressure often stems from a desire to fit in, gain approval, or avoid rejection.

Recognizing the Impact of Comparison

Comparison, on the other hand, involves measuring ourselves against others, often leading to feelings of inadequacy or superiority. In the age of social media, where carefully curated images and achievements are showcased, the tendency to compare ourselves to others has become more pronounced.

Strategies for Dealing with Peer Pressure

1. **Self-Awareness:** The first step in dealing with peer pressure is self-awareness. Understand your values, priorities, and boundaries. When you are clear about what matters to you, it becomes easier to resist pressures that don't align with your authentic self.
2. **Assertiveness:** Practice assertiveness by expressing your views, decisions, and boundaries confidently and respectfully. Assertive communication can help you stand your ground without succumbing to peer pressure.
3. **Selecting Supportive Relationships:** Surround yourself with friends and colleagues who respect your choices and values. Positive social connections can provide a buffer against negative peer pressure.

Strategies for Handling Comparison

1. **Practice Gratitude:** Cultivate a sense of gratitude for your unique qualities and accomplishments. Regularly remind yourself of your strengths and achievements to counteract feelings of inadequacy.

2. **Limit Social Media Exposure:** If social media triggers unhealthy comparison, consider reducing your exposure. Focus on meaningful offline connections and activities that bring you joy.
3. **Set Realistic Goals:** Establish personal goals that are meaningful to you, rather than chasing external markers of success. Define success on your terms.
4. **Mindfulness:** Use mindfulness techniques to stay present and avoid getting caught up in comparison. Mindful living encourages you to appreciate the here and now.
5. **Celebrate Differences:** Embrace diversity and appreciate the differences between you and others. Recognize that everyone has their own voyage and strengths.

The goal here is to help equip you with practical tools and exercises to navigate and overcome the challenges posed by peer pressure and comparison. By developing resilience and self-assurance, you can lead a more fulfilling life focused on what truly matters to you.

Maintaining Confidence in Your Priorities

Amid external pressures and societal expectations, maintaining confidence in your priorities is crucial for safeguarding your mental well-being. It's natural to question your choices when faced with pressure from peers or society. However, I feel that it's equally important to stand firm in your convictions. Sway when you need, but try not to make that the habit.

Embrace Self-Validation

One of the most effective ways to maintain confidence in your priorities is through self-validation. This involves acknowledging your choices and beliefs as valid and worthy, regardless of external opinions. Here's how to embrace self-validation:

1. **Self-Reflection:** Regularly reflect on your values, goals, and aspirations. Understand why these priorities matter to you and how they contribute to your well-being.
2. **Affirmations:** Use positive affirmations to reinforce your beliefs. Create statements that remind you of your values and the importance of staying true to them.
3. **Challenge Negative Self-Talk:** Be aware of any negative self-talk that questions your choices. Replace these thoughts with positive and affirming ones.

Seek Supportive Communities

Surrounding yourself with supportive communities can be a powerful source of validation. When you interact with people who share similar values and priorities, it reinforces your confidence in your choices. Consider the following:

1. **Join Like-Minded Groups:** Seek out groups, organizations, or communities that align with your values. Whether it's a hobby club, a professional network, or a social cause, connecting with like-minded individuals can boost your confidence.
2. **Share Your Goals:** Discuss your priorities and goals with trusted friends or mentors who can offer encouragement and validation. Sharing your aspirations with others who understand and support you can strengthen your

confidence.

Continuously Revisit Your Priorities

Priorities can evolve over time, and that's perfectly normal. It's essential to periodically revisit and reevaluate your priorities to ensure they align with your current values and life circumstances. Here's how to do it:

1. **Regular Check-Ins:** Set aside time for regular check-ins with yourself. Ask yourself whether your priorities still resonate with you and whether they contribute to your well-being.
2. **Adjust When Necessary:** Don't be afraid to adjust your priorities when needed. Life is dynamic, and your goals may shift as you grow and experience new things.

Cultivate Resilience

This plays a significant role in maintaining confidence in your priorities. It allows you to bounce back from external pressures and setbacks, which involves:

1. **Mindfulness and Self-Care:** Practice these to stay grounded and resilient in the face of external pressures. Taking care of your mental and emotional health is essential.
2. **Learn from Challenges:** View challenges and setbacks as opportunities for growth. They can reinforce your commitment to your priorities and make you more resilient in the long run.

By embracing self-validation, seeking supportive communities, continuously revisiting your priorities, and cultivating resilience, you can maintain unwavering confidence in what truly matters to you. This inner strength will serve as a solid foundation for navigating external pressures and leading a fulfilling life aligned with your priorities.

15

Unravel: A Comically Condensed Guide to Surviving Society's Side-Eye

So, you're living in a world where everyone and their grand-mother has an opinion about how you should live your life. From how you dress, to whom you should marry, and which overpriced coffee brand you should drink (because heaven forbid you like that "cheap" stuff).

The Not-So-Silent Pressure of Society: You see, society has this sneaky way of whispering (or sometimes shouting) what you *should* be doing. Sometimes it's cool, but most times it feels like that annoying neighbor who won't stop giving unsolicited gardening tips.

The Great Balancing Act: The epic battle - to fit in or be yourself? It's like choosing between eating the last slice of pizza in front of your dieting friend or politely pretending you're not hungry.

Say It with Me, "NO": You have a voice, so use it! If you don't want to do the cha-cha at Aunt Susan's fourth wedding, then don't. Assertiveness is the name, setting boundaries is the game.

A Compass for Your Life Choices: Put your values on the VIP list. By knowing what matters to YOU, you can dodge society's pesky pressures like Neo in The Matrix.

Talk It Out: If someone's pressuring you, have a chat. Maybe they don't realize they're being the human version of a pop-up ad.

Mirror Mirror on the Wall: Take a minute, reflect on what YOU want. Maybe it's peace, happiness, or just a donut. All are valid.

Stay in the Now: Remember to be present, and don't let FOMO mess with your mojo.

Peer Pressure & The Comparison Game: Remember back in school when everyone had those cool shoes, and you didn't? Yeah, that game's still around. But now, it's in "Who's got the fancier job or the cuter dog?" form. Keep in mind: Comparison is the thief of joy... and who needs a joy-stealer?

Hold On to Your Priorities: Lastly, be your biggest fan! Remind yourself that your choices are valid, find your tribe, and revisit your priorities if needed. Sometimes, they change – just like Aunt Susan's marital status.

Dance to your own tune, wear mismatched socks if you want, and always, ALWAYS prioritize that donut.

16

Building Resilience

"Why do we fall, sir? So we might learn to pick ourselves up."
– Alfred Pennyworth, Batman Begins

Developing

Emotional resilience is a valuable trait that empowers individuals to cope with life's challenges, bounce back from adversity, and maintain their mental well-being.

Understand and Accept Emotions

1. **Embrace Your Feelings:** The first step is to acknowledge and embrace your emotions. Understand that it's natural to experience a wide range of feelings, including sadness, anger, fear, and joy. Avoid judging yourself for how you feel.

2. **Practice Emotional Acceptance:** Rather than suppressing or denying your emotions, practice acceptance. Allow yourself to fully experience and express your feelings in healthy ways. Reflective writing, talking to a trusted friend,

or engaging in creative activities can help you process emotions.

Build a Support Network

1. **Seek Social Support:** Connect with friends, family, or support groups when you're going through challenging times. Sharing your feelings and concerns with others can provide emotional validation and comfort.
2. **Cultivate Positive Relationships:** Nurture supportive relationships in your life. Surrounding yourself with people who uplift and encourage you can enhance this fortitude.

Develop Coping Skills

1. **Learn Stress Management:** Stress is a common trigger for emotional distress. Learn stress management techniques such as deep breathing, meditation, or yoga to help regulate your emotions during stressful situations.
2. **Problem-Solving:** Develop problem-solving skills to address challenges effectively. Break down complex issues into smaller, manageable steps and seek solutions.

Foster a Growth Mindset

1. **View Challenges as Opportunities:** Cultivate a growth belief by viewing challenges as opportunities for personal growth. Instead of seeing setbacks as failures, see them as valuable learning experiences.
2. **Set Realistic Expectations:** Avoid setting unrealistic expectations for yourself. Recognize that being perfect is

unattainable, and it's okay (great, even) to make mistakes along the way.

Practice Self-Compassion

1. **Be Forgiving and Kind to Yourself:** Treat yourself with the same kindness, compassion, and respect you would offer to a friend. Avoid self-criticism and practice self-compassion, especially during difficult times.
2. **Challenge Negative Self-Talk:** Identify and challenge negative self-talk that can undermine your sturdiness. Replace negative thoughts with positive affirmations and realistic self-appraisals.

Developing everything above involves self-awareness, building supportive relationships, acquiring coping skills, fostering growth, and practicing self-compassion. By nurturing these aspects, you can better navigate life's ups and downs while safeguarding your mental well-being.

Overcoming Challenges on the Path to Prioritization

Developing emotional resilience and placing genuine priorities at the forefront of life can indeed be a captivating voyage, yet it is not devoid of its difficulties.

1. Resistance to Change

Challenge: One of the primary challenges is resistance to change. It can be difficult to break free from old habits and thought patterns.

Strategy: Embrace change gradually. Start by identifying small aspects of your life where you can allocate the importance of what matters. Over time, these small changes will accumulate, leading to significant shifts in your priorities.

2. External Pressures

Challenge: External pressures, such as societal expectations and peer influence, can push you to prioritize things that don't align with your true values.

Strategy: Strengthen your resolve and assertiveness. Learn to say "no" to external pressures that don't serve your well-being. Surround yourself with supportive individuals who respect your priorities.

3. Overwhelm

Challenge: The process of reevaluating your priorities and building resilience can sometimes feel overwhelming.

Strategy: Break it down into manageable steps. Focus on one aspect of your life at a time, whether it's relationships, work, or personal goals. This approach can make things more manageable and less daunting.

4. Fear of Missing Out (FOMO)

Challenge: The fear of missing out on opportunities or experiences can lead to overcommitment and spreading yourself too thin.

Strategy: Practice mindful decision-making. Before saying "yes" to something, pause and consider if it aligns with your true priorities. Remember that by saying "no" to some things, you make room for what truly matters.

5. Self-Doubt

Challenge: Self-doubt can undermine your efforts.

Strategy: Cultivate self-confidence. Celebrate your successes, no matter how small, and remind yourself of your strengths and capabilities. Surround yourself with supportive individuals who believe in you.

6. Perfectionism

Challenge: The pursuit of perfection can hinder prioritization as you may constantly strive to excel in every aspect of life.

Strategy: Embrace imperfection. Understand that it's okay to have flaws and make mistakes. Focus on progress, not perfection, and celebrate your achievements along the way.

7. Lack of Self-Care

Challenge: Neglecting yourself can deplete your emotional resilience.

Strategy: Place importance on all things YOU. Make time for activities that rejuvenate your mind and body, whether it's meditation, exercise, or simply taking moments of solitude.

Overcoming these challenges requires patience, self-compassion, and persistence. Remember that building up what truly matters is a process, and setbacks are a natural part of growth. By addressing these challenges with determination, you can continue on your path to total fulfillment.

Strengthening Your Mentality

Fostering resilience and giving precedence to what genuinely holds value in life are essential elements in elevating your mental outlook.

1. Mindfulness Meditation

Practice Mindfulness: Engaging in regular mindfulness meditation can help you stay grounded and centered. It enables you to become more aware of your thoughts and feelings, allowing you to make conscious choices about your priorities.

How to Start: Dedicate a few minutes each day to mindfulness meditation. Begin by focusing on your breath and gradually expand your awareness to your thoughts and sensations. Over time, this practice can help you better understand your priorities and manage stress.

2. Emotional Intelligence

Cultivate Emotional Intelligence: Developing emotional intelligence involves recognizing and understanding your emotions, as well as those of others. This skill can aid in making informed decisions about your priorities and responding effectively to challenges.

How to Cultivate It: Practice self-awareness by regularly checking in with your emotions. A diary can be a helpful tool for this. Additionally, actively listen to others and empathize with their feelings to enhance your emotional intelligence.

3. Positive Psychology

Embrace Positivity: This psychology focuses on strengths, virtues, and factors that contribute to a fulfilling life. Incorporate positive thinking and gratitude into your daily routine.

How to Apply It: Start a gratitude journal, where you jot down things you're thankful for each day. Surround yourself with positive influences, whether it's through books, podcasts, or uplifting conversations.

4. Self-Care

Prioritize: This is crucial for maintaining wellness. It involves activities that rejuvenate your mind and body, and reduce stress.

Incorporate: Identify practices that resonate with you, whether it's exercise, spending time in nature, reading, or enjoying hobbies. Schedule regular moments into your routine to ensure they become a priority.

5. Resilience-Building Activities

Build: Engage in activities that challenge and strengthen you. Facing and overcoming adversity can enhance your ability to prioritize effectively.

How to: Consider taking on new challenges or setting goals that align with your true priorities. These experiences can foster and reinforce your commitment to what matters most.

6. Seek Support

Reach Out: Don't hesitate to seek support from friends, family, or mental health professionals when needed. Sharing your life and thoughts with others can provide valuable insights and encouragement.

When to Seek Support: If you find yourself struggling with prioritization or facing significant obstacles, reaching out to a counselor, therapist, or support group can be instrumental.

By incorporating these strategies into your life, you can actively work on enhancing while progressing on your path. Strengthening your mental well-being will enable you to face challenges with greater clarity and make choices aligned with your true values and priorities.

17

Unravel: The Ultimate Guide to Bouncing Back & Bossing Up

Developing Emotional Resilience: Think of this as the gym for your feelings. We're getting emotionally swole here!

1. **Embrace Your Feelings** - You're human! You're gonna have feels. It's like the weather, sometimes sunny, sometimes stormy. No judging!
2. **Build a Support Network** - Get yourself an emotional A-team. Because who wants to go on an emotional rollercoaster alone?
3. **Develop Coping Skills** - The adult version of learning to ride a bike, but for your brain.
4. **Foster a Growth Mindset** - Look at those hurdles and go, "You're just a stepping stone, buddy!"
5. **Practice Self-Compassion** - Be your own hype-person. Pump up the jams... and the self-love.

Overcoming Challenges on the Path to Prioritization: The emotional equivalent of "Mario Kart" – watch out for those banana peels!

1. **Resistance to Change** - Old habits die hard, but we've got some respawn points up ahead.
2. **External Pressures** - Remember: Not everyone's a fan of pineapple on pizza, and that's okay!
3. **Overwhelm** - Baby steps. Imagine turning life's mountain into a molehill, one step at a time.
4. **FOMO** - The buffet of life is vast; it's okay to skip the salad sometimes.
5. **Self-Doubt** - Turn that inner critic into a motivational coach.
6. **Perfectionism** - Newsflash: Nobody's perfect! But we're all pretty darn awesome.
7. **Lack of Self-Care** - Recharge that emotional battery; you deserve it.

Strengthening Your Mental Wellness: It's like "The Sims", but it's your brain. Let's boost those stats!

1. **Mindfulness Meditation** - Like giving your brain a mini-vacation without the sunburn.
2. **Emotional Intelligence** - The emotional Olympics. Go for gold!
3. **Positive Psychology** - Your brain's daily dose of sunshine.
4. **Self-Care** - Because you're not a robot, even if you're powered by coffee.
5. **Resilience-Building Activities** - Get that mental six-pack!
6. **Seek Support** - Because sometimes, we need to tag in a teammate.

So, there you have it: the cool, quirky guide to bouncing back, shining bright, and making those emotional muscles dance!

85

18

Sustaining "I Don't Care" in Daily Life

"Who are we? Are we simply what others want us to be? Are destined to a fate beyond our control? Or can we evolve? Become... something more?"
– Jean Grey, X–Men: Dark Phoenix

Creating a Sustainable Mindset

As we near the culmination of our adventure, it's vital to discuss how to sustain all of this in your daily life. While you've learned valuable strategies and insights, maintaining this way of living requires intentional efforts. Let's work on creating a change that endures.

1. Embrace Adaptability

Stay Open to Change: Life is dynamic, and your priorities may shift over time. Embracing adaptability means recognizing that what matters most can evolve. It's not about rigidly adhering to one set of priorities but adapting to new circumstances.

Practice Flexibility: Cultivate a flexible perspective that allows you to adjust your priorities when necessary. This doesn't mean abandoning your principles but rather being responsive to the changing demands of life.

2. Consistent Self-Reflection

Regularly Assess Your Priorities: Just as you did earlier, continue to engage in self-reflection. Regularly assess your priorities to ensure they align with your values and current life circumstances.

Reflective Writing: Maintaining a journal or digital notes can be a valuable practice for ongoing self-reflection. Write about your changing priorities and how your choices continue to support your emotional health.

3. Set Boundaries

Protect Your Mental Space: Guard your mental well-being by setting and maintaining boundaries. Be clear about what you're willing to commit to and what you need to decline.

Practice Saying No: Continue to apply the art of saying 'No' to non-essential commitments. It's a skill that, when used thoughtfully, reinforces your dedication to prioritization.

4. Stay Connected to Your 'Why'

Remember Your Purpose: Reflect on the deeper reasons behind your decisions. Keep your 'why' at the forefront of your mind as a source of motivation.

Visual Reminders: Use visual cues, such as inspirational quotes or symbols, to remind yourself of your purpose and the benefits of prioritization. These reminders can reinforce your commitment.

5. Seek Support and Accountability

Engage with a Support System: Share with friends, family, or support groups who understand and appreciate your commitment.

Accountability Partners: Consider having an accountability partner who can help you stay on track. You can mutually support each other in your endeavors.

6. Celebrate Your Progress

Acknowledge Your Achievements: Celebrate your successes, no matter how small. Recognize the constructive impact your progress has had on your quality of life.

Rewards: Treat yourself to rewards as a way of acknowledging your progress. Positive reinforcement can encourage the continued practice of prioritization.

By creating a sustainable disposition, you'll be equipped to integrate this philosophy into your daily life effectively. This enduring commitment will not only benefit you but also those around you as you inspire them to focus on what truly matters in life.

Forming Healthy Habits to Support Your Priorities

Maintaining this involves more than just a mental shift; it requires the cultivation of healthy habits that align with your priorities.

1. Prioritize Self-Care

Daily Rituals: Dedicate time each day for practices that nourish your mind, body, and soul. This can include meditation, exercise, reading, or any activity that rejuvenates you.

Set Boundaries: Ensure that self-wellness is non-negotiable. Clearly define boundaries around your personal time and communicate these boundaries to others to protect your mental well-being.

2. Time Management

Effective Time Blocking: Use time-blocking techniques to allocate focused periods for your top priorities. Create a daily or weekly schedule that reflects your commitment to what truly matters.

Eliminate Time Wasters: Identify and eliminate activities that drain your time and energy without contributing to your well-being or goals. This includes excessive screen time, mindless scrolling, or unproductive meetings.

3. Mindful Decision-Making

Pause and Reflect: Before committing to new tasks or obligations, pause to reflect on how they align with your priorities. Mindful decision-making ensures that you stay true to your values.

Practice Saying No: Continue practicing assertiveness and saying 'No' to requests or commitments that don't serve your priorities. Politely decline and offer alternatives when necessary.

4. Digital Detox

Screen Time Reduction: Limit your screen time, especially on social media and apps that can be distracting. Consider designated tech-free periods to regain focus and mental clarity.

Unsubscribe and Unfollow: Remove excess of your digital life by unsubscribing from irrelevant emails and unfollowing accounts that don't align with your priorities or values.

5. Gratitude and Reflection

Daily Gratitude: Incorporate a daily gratitude practice into your routine. Reflect on the things that you are thankful for, reinforcing your appreciation for what truly matters.

Regular Review: Periodically review your priorities and how well you've aligned your life with them. This ongoing reflection helps you stay on track and make necessary adjustments.

6. Positive Affirmations

Affirm Your Priorities: Create affirmations that reinforce your commitment to your priorities. Repeating these affirmations daily can strengthen your resolve.

Visualization: Visualize yourself living a life centered around what truly matters. This mental imagery can motivate and remind you of your goals.

By forming healthy habits that support your priorities, you'll not only sustain the 'I Don't Care' mindset but also enhance your overall well-being. These habits act as the building blocks of a fulfilling and balanced life where priority rules.

Celebrating

As you continue, it's essential to acknowledge and celebrate yourself. Celebrating your progress can boost your motivation, reinforce your commitment, and bring a sense of accomplishment to your path. Here's how you can celebrate:

1. Milestone Recognition

Take a moment to recognize and celebrate your achievements,

no matter how small or significant they may be. These milestones could include:

- Successfully saying 'No' to unimportant commitments.
- Establishing a consistent self-care routine.
- Accomplishing personal or professional goals aligned with your priorities.

2. Self-Reflection

Engage in periodic self-reflection to assess your growth and development. Ask yourself questions like:

- How has my mental well-being improved?
- In what ways have I become more aligned with my priorities?
- What good changes have I noticed in my life?

3. Gratitude Practice

Continue to practice gratitude for the journey itself. Recognize the value of prioritizing and the impact it has had on your life.

4. Treat Yourself

Treat yourself to something special as a reward for your dedication to mental well-being. It could be a relaxing spa day, a favorite meal, or any activity that brings you joy.

5. Set New Goals

After celebrating your progress, set new goals that align with your evolving priorities. This continuous growth and adaptation will keep your cognitive balance dynamic and fulfilling.

6. Practice Self-Compassion

Be kind to yourself and acknowledge that setbacks are a natural part of life. Instead of dwelling on setbacks, focus on how you can learn from them and continue moving forward.

Celebrating yourself is an important aspect of life in general. It reinforces the positive changes you've made in your life and motivates you to continue focusing on what truly matters. Remember that your progress is yours, and every step forward is a reason to celebrate.

19

Unravel: How to Keep Not Caring (But in a Good Way!)

Embrace Adaptability: Life's like a game of Twister. Sometimes your left hand's on red, and other times it's on green. So, stay flexible and keep your balance!

Consistent Self-Reflection: Think of yourself as a smartphone. Every now and then, you need a software update. Journaling? It's like your personal cloud storage - back yourself up!

Set Boundaries: Guard your mental castle! Think of saying 'No' as your drawbridge - lower it for the friendly villagers, raise it for the dragons.

Stay Connected to Your 'Why': Stick a post-it note on your forehead if you must! Keep your purpose fresh and, well, sticky.

Seek Support and Accountability: It's like gym buddies but for your brain. Make sure they don't let you skip "mental wellness day"!

Celebrate Your Progress: It's like getting a gold star in kindergarten, but fancier. Every step counts!

Habit-Forming Time!

Prioritize Yourself: Pamper yourself like the royalty you are. A crown of self-care, please!

Time Management: Be the boss of your 24 hours. And hey, if you can find where those missing socks from the laundry go in the process, let us know!

Digital Detox: Go on a tech diet. Less digital junk, more mental munch!

Gratitude and Reflection: Count your blessings. Maybe not sheep, those are for bedtime.

Positive Affirmations: Pep talk yourself like you're both the coach and the star player. Score!

The Grand Finale: Celebrate Your 'I Don't Care' Gala!

Milestone Recognition: Got through a meeting without daydreaming about pizza? That's a win!

Self-Reflection: It's like taking a selfie but for your soul. Find your good side!

Treat Yourself: Because you're a rock star, and rock stars get treats. No autographs, please.

Set New Goals: Set 'em up and knock 'em down. You got this!

Practice Self-Compassion: Bad days happen. It's okay. Hug yourself (literally or metaphorically)!

And that's it, folks! The keys to not caring like a champ, while also caring about the right stuff. Keep rockin' and rollin' through life!

20

Your Mind, Your Power: Wrapping It Up

Throughout our journey in this book, there are truths I've inherently understood, almost as if I was built to navigate life's stresses with a different compass. It's like I was programmed to remain unflustered, reserving my energy for moments that truly mattered. As we conclude, I want to share a few pillars that have been indispensable for me:

1. **Minimalistic Living**: Interestingly, my tryst with minimalism doesn't apply to my love for electronics and comic figures (we all have our indulgences, don't we?). By cutting out the excess in other areas, I've found serenity and focus.
2. **Prioritizing Values**: Living a life that aligns with what I genuinely find important has been a game-changer. It's like setting the GPS of your life to a destination that resonates with your soul.
3. **Introspection**: The act of self-reflection is akin to having a conversation with oneself. It's been a cornerstone for my personal growth and has significantly enhanced the quality of my relationship. And yes, being married to a therapist

gives me an added advantage!

4. **Unwavering Convictions**: I've learned the art of standing my ground. Peer pressure, like a gusty wind, might try to sway me, but like a sturdy tree, I remain rooted.

While the above points have played monumental roles in my life, there's one sanctuary that was not touched upon in previous chapters but deserves its spotlight: **The Gym**.

My rendezvous with the gym isn't just about lifting weights or clocking miles; it's my form of meditation. Each time workday stressors built up, the gym became my escape, a place to channel that energy and transform it. The result? A post-workout euphoria, a sense of accomplishment, and the reassurance that I was doing something constructive for my well-being.

In essence, never underestimate the power of consistent exercise. It's not just a workout for the body but a therapy for the mind.

As we get to the conclusion of this book, remember that your mental and emotional well-being is a journey, not a destination. Find your anchors, embrace what resonates with you, and most importantly, prioritize yourself. Your mind, your power. Own it.

21

Conclusion

"It is not our abilities that show what we truly are ... it is our choices." – Dumbledore, Harry Potter and the Chamber of Secrets

Recap of Key Takeaways

As we conclude, let's reflect on the key takeaways that have guided you on your path to inner peace:

1. Prioritization Is Essential

Understanding what truly matters in your life is fundamental to your mental well-being. Prioritization allows you to focus your time, energy, and attention on what aligns with your values and brings you fulfillment.

2. The 'I Don't Care' Mindset

This is not about indifference; it's a conscious choice to let go of unimportant matters that drain your mental resources. It empowers you to say 'No' when necessary and make room for what matters most.

3. Self-Reflection

Regular self-reflection is a valuable tool for understanding your priorities and assessing your progress. It helps you stay aligned with your values and make necessary adjustments along the way.

4. Mindfulness

Practicing mindfulness enables you to live in the present moment, reducing stress and anxiety. It allows you to fully engage with what matters, fostering a deeper connection to your priorities.

5. Resilience

Building emotional resilience is crucial for navigating challenges and setbacks. Having this helps you bounce back from adversity and maintain your mental well-being.

6. Sustainable Habits

Creating sustainable habits that support your priorities ensures long-term success. These habits include self-care routines, assertiveness, and effective boundary-setting.

7. Celebration

Don't forget to celebrate! Acknowledge your achievements, no matter how small, and use them as motivation to continue prioritizing your well-being.

8. Continuous Growth

Your priorities may evolve over time, and that's okay. Embrace change and adapt your frame of mind to align with your shifting values and goals.

9. Self-Compassion

Be kind to yourself as you focus on making changes. Understand that setbacks are normal, and self-compassion will help you persevere.

10. Community

Sharing your experiences with a supportive community can provide encouragement and valuable insights. Don't hesitate to seek support when needed.

As you move forward, embrace the principles of not caring, mindfulness, resilience, and self-compassion to continue living a life focused on what truly matters.

Encouragement for Continued Growth

As you reach the conclusion of this book, it's important to acknowledge that this path is ongoing. Here's some encouragement to inspire your continued growth:

Embrace Change

Change is a constant in life. Your priorities may shift as you grow and evolve. Embrace these changes and view them as opportunities for personal and mental growth. Flexibility and adaptability are key components of a healthy mind.

Practice Self-Compassion

Remember to be kind to yourself. Everyone faces challenges, setbacks, and moments of doubt. Self-compassion allows you to treat yourself with the same kindness and understanding that you would offer to a friend. It's okay to stumble along the way; what matters is how you respond.

Seek Support

Building a support network is essential. Surround yourself with people who understand and encourage you. Seek out friends, family members, or professionals who can provide guidance, lend an empathetic ear, or offer valuable insights.

Celebrate Milestones

Celebrate your achievements, no matter how small they may seem. Recognizing your progress reinforces your commitment to understanding what matters most in your life. Celebrations can also serve as motivation to keep moving forward.

Continuously Learn

Stay curious and open to learning. This is a lifelong goal, and there is always room for growth and improvement. Explore new techniques, resilience–building strategies, and ways to enhance your prioritization skills.

Pay It Forward

Share your experiences and insights with others. What you do can inspire and support those around you who may also be seeking a more fulfilling and balanced life. Being a source of encouragement for others can be deeply rewarding.

Reflect Regularly

Make self–reflection a habit. Periodically check in with yourself to ensure that your priorities align with your values and goals. This practice will help you stay on course and make any necessary adjustments.

Stay Committed

Remember that prioritization is an ongoing commitment to your mental well-being. There may be moments of doubt or temptation to revert to old habits, but stay true to your path. The 'I Don't Care' mindset will continue to guide you toward a life focused on what truly matters.

Gratitude

Cultivate gratitude. Every step you take is an opportunity for personal growth and fulfillment. Be thankful for the opportunity to live a life with intention and purpose.

Your Adventure, Your Path

Embrace your individuality, and don't compare your progress to others. Trust in your ability to set in order what matters most and create a life that aligns with your values.

A Reminder to Prioritize Yourself

In closing, let this be a gentle reminder: Your mental health should always be a priority in your life. All that you've undertaken by exploring this philosophy and the principles outlined is a testament to your commitment to a fulfilling and balanced life.

As you navigate the complexities of modern life, remember that it's not selfish or indulgent to prioritize your mental well-being. It's a fundamental necessity. When you take care of your mental health, you equip yourself to face challenges with resilience, make decisions aligned with your values, and cultivate meaningful relationships.

In the hustle and bustle of daily life, it's easy to get caught up in the demands and expectations of others. But always take a step back, pause, and reflect on what truly matters to you. Let this reflection guide your choices, actions, and point of view.

The power of those few words lie in its ability to free you from the weight of unimportant matters, allowing you to focus your energy on what truly enriches your life. Use it as a mantra to reinforce your commitment.

Incorporate the practices of mindfulness, resilience, and assertiveness into your daily routine. Continuously strive to align your priorities with your values and goals. Seek support when needed, and never underestimate the importance of self-compassion.

Health, in all forms, is not a destination but a lifelong exploration. It's a roller-coaster that offers growth, self-discovery, and a deeper connection to what matters most in your life. Embrace this with open arms, and may it lead you to a life filled with purpose, joy, and fulfillment.

As you close this book (or swipe the page), carry with you the knowledge that you have gained. You have the capacity to create a life that aligns with your values and brings you lasting happiness. The choice is yours, and it's a choice worth making every day.

Thank you for being part of this exploration. May you continue life with intention, care, and the unwavering belief that you deserve a life filled with what truly matters.

And remember, the art of not caring is truly the best self-care!

-Chase

About Me

During the workweek, I wear the hat of a computer programmer and developer, where precision is my creed and logic, my language. But hey, I'm not all 1s and 0s; I'm also an avid gamer, a cinephile, a music enthusiast, and a fitness fanatic. It's this fusion of the analytical and the imaginative that inspired me to pen these words.

I'm also a passionate advocate for mental health. This book is more than just a literary debut (aside from an attempt at a novel); it's a heartfelt exploration of the intersections between logic, creativity, and the crucial realm of mental well-being.

In the virtual realms of video games, I've battled dragons, solved puzzles, and conquered galaxies—all in the pursuit of that sweet, sweet victory. Movies? Well, they're my alternate reality, a canvas where dreams and stories come to life. Music is my trusted companion on this journey, setting the tone for every chapter of life. And working out? It's not just about flexing muscles; it's about flexing my mind and body in harmony.

But what sets me apart is my unwavering belief in the power of "Meh." Yes, you read that right—Meh, the zen philosophy of not sweating the small stuff, and trust me, there's plenty of it in our tech-driven world. This book is a chronicle of my journey to find balance in the chaos, to embrace the analytical mind and the imaginative soul, and to help you find your unique equilibrium.

www.ingramcontent.com/pod-product-compliance
Lightning Source LLC
Chambersburg PA
CBHW050924260726

48660CB00001B/386